EXERCISES TIGER and FABIUS

*An illustrated account of the American Forces
assault exercises held at Slapton Sands in 1944
as a rehearsal for part of the D-Day landings in France.*

Arthur L. Clamp

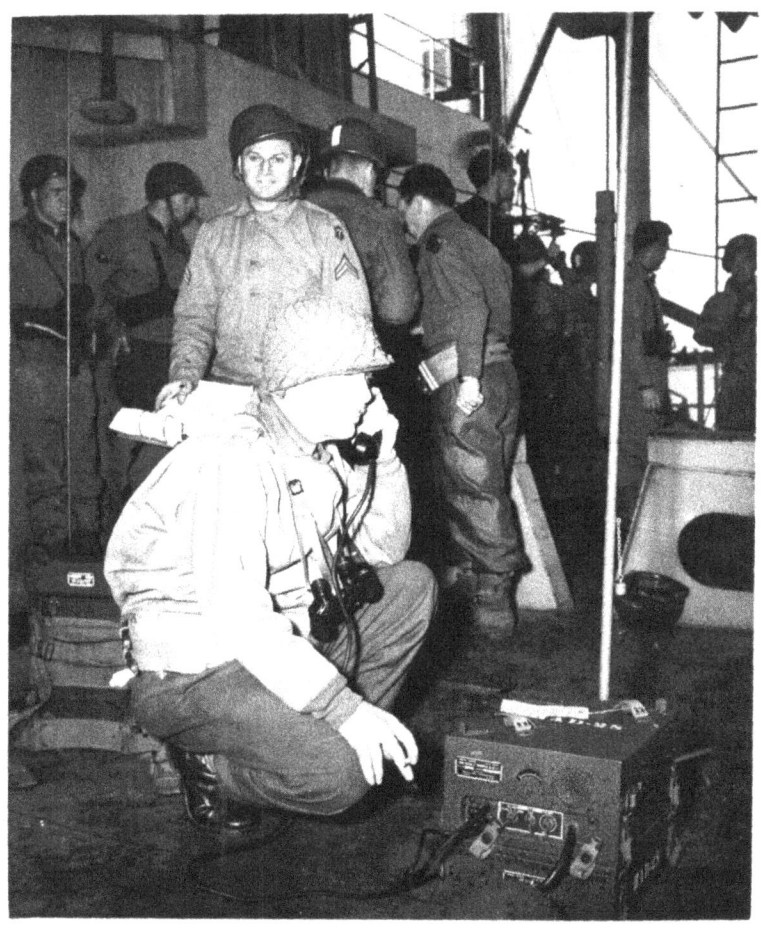

Major General Raymond O. Barton, C.G., Infantry Division,
issuing instructions for the invasion manoeuvre "Exercise Tiger"
off the coast of South Devon on 27th April, 1944.

This version of the book is virtually as originally published.
There are now additional pages at the back providing information about the author.

The republishing project is being managed by Arthur's grandson, Steven Gibson. We aim to find all the research
that he was involved in publishing, preserving it for the next generation as part of 'The Clamp Collection'.

Introduction

Thirty years and more have passed since American combat troops used Slapton Sands and the neighbouring countryside for full scale rehearsal exercises in preparation for the D-Day landings in Normandy, France, which eventually led to the collapse of Hitler's Germany and peace in Europe. This area of coast and land was selected as one of a series of training grounds which, in this case, was used because it closely resembled the landing beach, code named *Utah Beach*, situated on the Cherbourg peninsula. The American forces stationed in Devon and Cornwall were known as *U Force*, and were part of a much larger invading force which landed in France at five points on the 6th June, 1944.

This historic event and its subsequent success marked the closing stages of the Second World War. Never before had such a large and complex number of troops, drawn from different nationalities, assembled in this country for the purpose of launching a major cross-channel attack on an enemy and it is very unlikely that an event of this scale will ever be possible again as the means of detection by satellites would soon bring it to the attention of an opposing army.

Slapton Sands and its immediate land area played a very important part in this enterprise. Many people still recall the evacuation of all its inhabitants and livestock from many farms, villages and homesteads and the appearance of U.S. troops engaged in realistic exercises in which many casualties occurred. This brief episode in the life of the South Hams has not been forgotten and enquiries from visiting Americans still show a continuing interest in this event.

In the preparation of this account of the exercises I was greatly helped by the American military archives in Washington, U.S.A., from which source came the photographs. My thanks go to them and to many others working in Devon and London libraries who gave advice and time willingly. Lastly this title is dedicated to those who lost their lives during the preparations for D-Day and to the local people whose homes and livelihood were disrupted during 1943 and 1944.

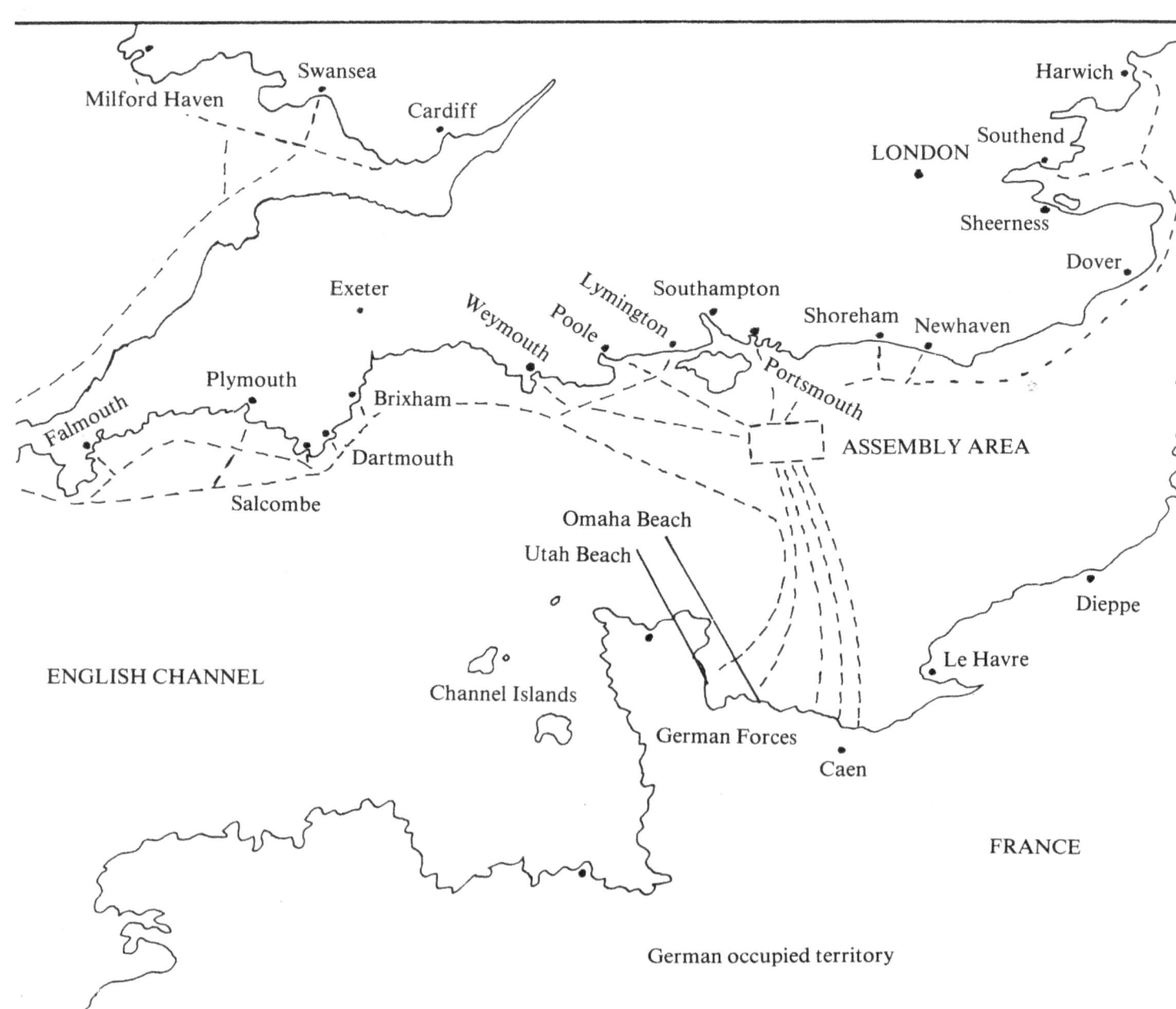

German occupied territory

Preparations for D-Day Invasion

It was becoming evident to people in England during the middle years of the war that sooner or later an attack would take place somewhere on European soil to bring to an end Hitler's occupation of the Continent and his own downfall. Extensive fighting had been taking place on the Russian Front for two years and more and they were, quite naturally, pressing the Allies to open up a Second Front along the Western coast of Europe.

The idea of a cross-channel invasion of Europe had been considered as early as 1940 but it was not until January, 1943, that, at a conference of Heads of Allied Governments in Casablanca, a firm decision was taken to launch a Second Front in the spring of 1944. Hitler's forces in North Africa were on the retreat by this time, a considerable build up of troops and military equipment was taking place in England, the Americans were shipping vast supplies from the States and troops were becoming available for other duties away from the Mediterranean theatre of war.

This enormous build up of men and supplies was an exceptionally well planned operation the purpose of which was only fully known to a few senior military and Government personnel. Co-ordination between hundreds of units, thousands of troops, both land and air based, soon resulted in England almost becoming a vast arsenal of supply dumps which were very carefully camouflaged and scattered throughout the land. Troops of many nationalities were involved and support was being planned by the French resistance movement behind the German lines.

This final assemblage of forces for the planned invasion was immense. Nothing had ever occurred on this scale in England; the whole country was poised for an attack on what was known as the Fortress of Europe. There were in readiness 1,213 warships, including 7 battleships and 23 cruisers, 4,126 landing craft, 1,600 ancillary and merchant ships, 11,500 aircraft and 3,500 gliders. The allied army numbered 3½ million men of whom 1½ million were Americans. Nearly 150,000 troops were to be put ashore on D-Day alone. Almost the full length of the southern coast was declared a military zone through which movement of civilians was restricted and information about any aspect of military matters kept secret.

During the early months of 1944 plans were well in hand for the overall structure of the invasion plan and the preparation of land and air based troop movements leading to various departure points facing the English Channel. *Operation Overlord* was to be undertaken by five assault forces, two comprising of American troops and three of British and other troops. Five designated areas between Cherbourg and Le Havre along the coast of Normandy were code named and allocated one to each force. Airborne troops would be the first to land in France paving the way for the full scale landings in the early hours of 6th June, 1944, a date that had yet to be finally arranged.

The American forces were mainly situated in the West Country and divided in two assault groups 'U' and 'O' (to land at *Utah* and *Omaha* Beaches) followed by force 'B' which was mainly in camp around Falmouth and Plymouth. Assault force 'U' was concentrated around Salcombe, Dartmouth and Brixham in South Devon and assault force 'O' was in the Portland, Weymouth and Poole areas of Dorset. The U.S. 1st Division was responsible for the Omaha landing and the U.S. 4th Division for the Utah landing. The U.S. Airborne Divisions 82nd and 101st were to be dropped inland from these beaches during the cover of darkness preceding the first light landings.

The British, Canadian and other troops were divided into assault forces 'G', 'J' and 'S' which were to land on beaches, code named Gold, Juno and Sword some miles east of the American landings. They were mainly stationed in the Hampshire area at Southampton, Portsmouth, Shoreham and Newhaven.

Both American and British airborne troops, aircraft and gliders were working towards a state of readiness on permanent and temporary airfields throughout southern England. These would be the first troops to land in occupied France and their task

General Eisenhower smiling at the invasion's success.

was to capture certain key positions close to the beach landings and then to link up with ground troops after beacheads had been established and a way made clear for the follow up forces to move inland.

The command structure of this giant operation came under General Eisenhower who was the Supreme Allied Commander assisted by Air Chief Marshall Sir Arthur Teddar as his deputy. The American Western Naval Task Force came under Rear-Admiral A. G. Kirk, U.S.N., aboard U.S.S. *Augusta* while Rear-Admiral D. P. Moon, U.S.N., was responsible for assault force 'U' and Rear-

Admiral J. L. Hall, Jr., U.S.N., for assault force 'O'. General Sir Bernard Montgomery, back from the successful North African campaign, took charge of the overall landings and breakthrough inland.

The stage for launching the cross-channel invasion was nearly ready. The original plans had been modified by Montgomery and the final ones were accepted on 15th May, 1944, at his headquarters in Hammersmith. The audience, which included Winston Churchill and King George VI, heard that the landings were to be made by two divisions of the U.S. First Army under the command of Lieut-General Omar N. Bradley and three divisions of the British 2nd Army led by Lieut-General Sir Miles Dempsey.

As the days and weeks passed during the spring of 1944 troops and supplies were being assembled in concentration areas, equipment not required for the immediate landings was left behind and by the 26th May the actual assault troops were camped in marshalling areas. These were sealed in camps where briefings took place although the exact place and time of the invasion was still withheld. Up to this date only senior staff were aware of the precise nature of the attack and this was only made known to the troops when they were crossing the Channel. Some 170 million maps, diagrams and plans were issued during the last hours before the French coast was reached.

Special points of embarkation had been set aside and "hards" were constructed over which heavy vehicles and equipment could be taken into landing ships and craft. A 130 of these had been laid over beaches which enabled tanks, lorries, etc., to cross safely. In order to keep the equipment and supplies dry during the crossing, every major item had to be waterproofed, and then de-waterproofed after landing. The actual day and time for the invasion had still to be finalised as weather conditions would play an important part in the success of this operation.

Unsettled weather conditions did cause some delay at the last moment. It had been decided to time the invasion for first light on the 5th June, 1944, but a last minute forecast caused a change of date. However, with some troops already set to sea and a break in the weather was anticipated *Operation Overlord* was set on course for landing at 06.30 hours on Tuesday, 6th June, 1944.

American infantry on one of their last exercises in southern England a few weeks before D-Day.

Landing Crafts

The very large operation required a number of specialised craft for carrying troops and equipment across the Channel. *Landing craft infantry (large)* was designed for holding 200 men and had a speed of 15 knots. *Landing craft tank* was a specially adapted craft designed to carry heavy tanks or vehicles right up to a beach. *Landing craft assault* was an armoured craft of 10 tons capable of holding 36 men and their equipment and landing them over a ramp in its bow. *Landing craft vehicle* and *Landing craft personnel* are, as their names indicate, craft adapted for particular uses taking loads right up to the beaches.

Allied Invasion Chiefs in conference. Left to right: General Bradley, Admiral Ramsey, Air Chief Marshal Tedder, General Eisenhower, General Montgomery, Air Chief Marshal Leigh-Mallory, and General Smith.

The Evacuation of the South Hams

As part of the necessary preparation for the successful invasion of German occupied France, it was vitally important that all troops had to undergo a series of training schedules and then fullscale exercises under conditions as near resembling those of the five landing points in Normandy as possible.

Slapton Sands and the immediate landward area was one of four major exercise areas designated for specialised use with live ammunition. Hayling Island, Bracklesham Bay and Littlehampton were the three other main training areas which came under strict military rule from the end of 1943 to the autumn of 1944. Slapton Sands with its small ley, low cliffs at either end of the flat coast road was not all that dissimilar from the beach and cliffs code named *Utah* west of the River Vire in Normandy. It was smaller, had fewer fortifications but was well away from German planes crossing the Channel towards the more populated areas of England.

A notice of requisition was passed to the Devon County Council under the Defence Regulations Act of 1939 specifying that a certain area of the South Hams was to be fully evacuated of civilians and livestock by the 20th December, 1943. This gave six weeks notice for the moving of about 750 families, comprising about 3,000 people, 180 farms, villages, shops, etc. Some 30,000 acres would have to be cleared in these weeks so that troops could move in and start setting up camps, defence points and ringing the area with guards.

The area (see map) took in the villages of Torcross, Stokenham, Chillington, Sherford, East Allington, Blackawton, Strete and Slapton and many hamlets. The requisitioned land covered the coast from just north of Strete to just south of Torcross and formed a diamond like area. All movable possessions from homes, shops and farms were to be taken and usuable crops still in the land could be removed. Nothing was to be left apart from empty buildings and churches.

Meetings were convened in the various village halls telling people of the plans and how they could get help in the form of packing cases, transport and food and assistance with the actual work of handling heavy furniture, farm equipment and livestock. The people were naturally taken back by the order to evacuate but it was wartime and almost anything could take place. Plymouth had suffered a devastating blitz, young children were living in the area as evacuees, husbands were at war so this move, it was explained, however difficult, upsetting and inconvenient it would be was necessary and would make a very practical contribution to training troops to win the war.

Two information centres were set up at Blackawton and Stokenham and staffed by the Women's Voluntary Service. Help was forthcoming from many people throughout Devon and offers of accommodation given while farmers roundabout

shared fields and equipment with those who lost their land. Advice was given about obtaining help, seeking alternative accommodation and storing furniture and goods. Emergency kitchens were able to supply meals to those in the middle of moving; transport, in one or another, was made available for moving out tons of domestic and farming goods to many parts of the West Country.

There were, of course, difficulties especially with the elderly folk many of whom had never left the area before and with sick people where it was necessary to find them beds in nearby hospitals. These and many other problems were overcome by a willingness on most people's part to pull together and make the most of it. The war was on and this was one consequence of the times.

As the few weeks passed so the land and villages took on a deserted appearance. The once crowded roads down to the shore, the busy farms, the cattle grazing the fields, the people talking in the village shops were to be no more. The large villages were soon empty then came the many farms and finally the isolated houses. The various churches had to be cleared of valuables and very old furnishings. No guarantee that anything left would be undamaged during the exercises. Treasures such as crucifixes, silver crosses and plateware were carefully packed by experts and monuments, windows and fittings were protected by sandbags. Almost all the churches had a lot of old and fragile woodwork. This required very careful dismantling and packing helped in many cases by the incoming U.S. troops. The inns closed their doors for the last time and the cellars were emptied of their stocks of cyder and beer.

During the last few days of the evacuation sentries came into the area, American officials checked on the clearing operation, the last people left taking with them as much of their crops as possible and finally the centres closed and the volunteers moved out. A silence fell over the area, an uncanny feeling that this was the lull before the storm. Weeds soon appeared in unattended gardens and fields, hedgerows grew out of shape and houses, farms and other buildings quickly gathered dust during those last days of 1943.

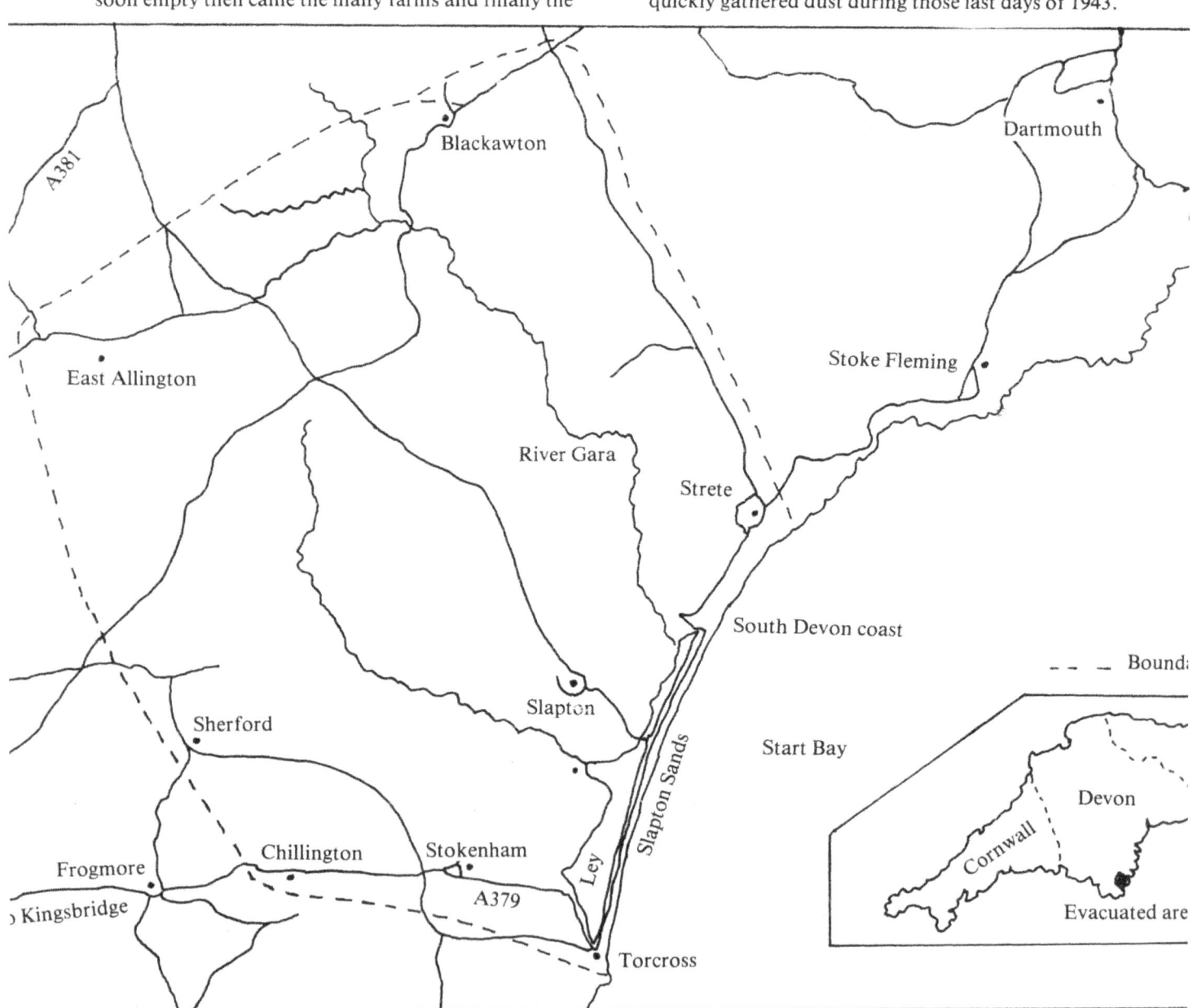

U.S. Troop Exercises at Slapton Sands

During the opening weeks of 1944 Slapton Sands and area became the scene of great activity with troops coming in setting up posts, defence positions, converting some buildings to observation points and preparing obstacles along the beach and main road. The whole area soon took on the appearance of a large military range with guns in position, signal stations working, encampments for the troops and vehicles and supplies stored in depots.

The area had been sealed off completely to civilians and only those with special permits were allowed in or could work close by such as coastguards and local homeguards who were responsible for maintaining watch along the nearby cliffs.

It soon became apparent to people living close by that something special was going to happen here as the large number of troops and their supplies could not be completely kept out of sight when approaching the area. People were asked not to say anything to anyone about what they saw or heard and troops when allowed out of the area while off duty were likewise warned of casual talk.

There were also American troops with equipment and supplies stationed at nearby Salcombe, Dartmouth and Brixham but these local areas were not barred to civilians in the same way as the Slapton Sands area. There was plenty of movement between these local stations and many lanes and some roads had to be widened or straightened to cope with the large amount of transport and the size of many military vehicles. It became very clear after a month or two that Slapton would play a very special role in the preparation of forces for the invasion of Europe although at this point in time nobody knew of the exact intentions of all this military activity or when it would leave South Devon on its mission to clear Europe of Hitler's troops.

TOP SECRET

SUPREME HEADQUARTERS
ALLIED EXPEDITIONARY FORCE
C-3 Division

SHAEF/18231/Ops   18th March, 1944

SUBJECT: Large scale exercises

TO   : Allied Naval Commander XF,
            Commander-in-Chief, 21 Army Group,
            Air Commander-in-Chief, AEAF.

Reference X/0840/10 dated 8th March, 1944.

The Supreme Commander approves the schedule of exercises proposed by you in the letter under reference.

In order to assist plan 'FORTITUDE' you should endeavour, paying due regard to security, to make the large scale exercise (Exercise 'FABIUS') appear similar in character to the mounting of 'NEPTUNE' in those aspects which are apparent to enemy air reconnaisance and 'Y' intercept service.

                                    W. B. Smith,
                              Lieutenant General, US Army,
                                    Chief of Staff.

TOP SECRET

Troops of assault forces "U" and "O" stationed throughout the West Country were, during the early months of 1944, engaged in a series of very specialised training schemes at selected areas in Devon and Cornwall and along the coast towards Weymouth. These minor exercises were to test various pieces of equipment, procedures and the demolition of obstacles prior to staging a small landing or attacking a given target. One centre was at Braunton in North Devon, the United States Assault Training Centre, where infantry battalions undertook training in amphibious techniques, the reduction of "hedgehog" defences on beaches and attack tactics on fortified gun emplacements. These exercises were designed to test the efficiency of equipment and the effectiveness of small battalions of troops from which

experience was gained and some modifications made to equipment and methods of attack.

Meanwhile other troops were undergoing a series of hardening exercises on Dartmoor, a terrain which is difficult to cross especially under poor weather conditions when much of it can soon be covered in cloud. Every effort was made during these preliminary exercises to make them as realistic as possible through the use of live ammunition over the heads and immediately in front of troops.

At the completion of these localised movements Divisional Commanders were briefed on the next stage of training when the whole of assault forces "U" and "O" would engage in two separate full scale rehearsals at Slapton. Towards the end of April, 1944, *Operation Tiger* took place with force "U" and at the beginning of May *Operation Fabius* followed with

force "O". Both exercises were conducted under conditions simulating as closely as possible those expected in the actual D-Day landings. The troops were not informed of the real purpose of these although no doubt many guessed their true nature and some, it was reported, actually thought that when they had embarked and set course towards the South Devon coast they were on the way to France. The rehearsals were organised and conducted with all the detail and thoroughness of the actual invasion. Landing craft were assigned from various bases along the South Devon coast to carry troops and equipment on a sea journey of the same length and time as it would take to cross the Channel to France. Assault teams were made up and plans of the rehearsal, objectives to reach and the conditions under which the troops would be landing were made known.

SUPREME HEADQUARTERS
ALLIED EXPEDITIONARY FORCE
G-3 Division

SHAEF/23036/8/Trg   19 April 1944.

Subject: Exercise Tiger.

To:

    1. Exercise TIGER will involve the concentration, marshalling and embarkation of troops in the TOR BAY - PLYMOUTH area, and a short movement by sea under the control of the U.S. Navy, disembarkation with Naval and Air support at SLAPTON SANDS, a beach assault using service ammunition, the securing of a beachhead and a rapid advance inland.

    2. Major troop units are the VII Corps Troops, 4th Infantry Division, the 101st and 82nd Airborne Divisions, 1st Engineer Special Brigade, Force "U" and supporting Air Force units.

    3. During the period H-60 to H-45 minutes, fighter-bombers attack inland targets on call from the 101st AB Div and medium bombers attack three targets along the beach. Additional targets will be bombed by both fighter-bombers and medium bombers on call from ground units. Simulated missions will also be flown with the target areas marked by smoke pots.

    4. Naval vessels fire upon beach obstacles from H-50 to H-hour. Smoke may be used during the latter part of the naval bombardment both from Naval craft by 4.2" chemical mortars and at H-hour by planes, if weather conditions are favourable. Naval fire ceases at H-hour.

    5. The schedule of the exercise is as follows:

	22 April	Move to marshalling area commences.
D-Day	27 April	101st AB Div simulates landing. Preparatory bombardment by air and navy. Assault landing and advance of 4th Div.
	28-29 April	Advance of 4th Div & 101st AB Div continues. 82nd AB Div simulates landing, secure and holds objective.

    (Exercise terminates on 29 April)

    6. Joining instructions will be issued later.

W. R. PIERCE,
Colonel, G.S.C.,
Chief, Training, Sub-Section.

TOP SECRET
This paper must not be taken out of this Headquarters except as laid down in Para. 27, SHAEF Inter-Division Standing Security Regulations dated 9 February 1944.

Within the very tight restrictions imposed by security along the whole of the English coast both exercises were to embody every detail that would be required for the landings on the Normandy coast. Troops were assembled in marshalling areas, briefed on their mission, taken to loading hards and assigned to the appropriate landing craft. The number of men involved and the manner of their grouping and use of equipment was exactly as it would be for the real operation. A course was set along the south coast to approximate the length of the channel crossing and the timing of departure and subsequent landing on the pebble beach at Slapton was to follow the prepared schedule for D-Day. The sea journey was to be covered by air support and under the control of the U.S. Navy.

Disembarkation was also to be covered with air and naval support preceeded by

preparatory bombardment of the coastal area while the troops were being taken towards the shore in the early hours of their assigned landing day. Naval vessels would be stationed in Start Bay to soften up positions along Slapton beach minutes before the troops were to land.

So the scene was set in this part of normally quiet Devon when people would often look out to sea and watch a few fishing boats go by or an occasional large boat on the horizon. Many of them must have been very surprised to see numerous landing craft coming into the area during the last days of April and the first few of May during that eventful year of 1944. If the craft could not be seen from away from the coast the attack by ships and planes could certainly be heard for many miles over the Devon countryside. It would be soon obvious to the local people that a large scale military exercise was under way and that this was a foretaste of a later event to take place somewhere in Europe.

A variety of objectives had been set up along the beach and its immediate landward area. These included gun emplacements, defended buildings, a dummy aerodrome and other features to resemble those to be expected on the Normandy coast. The beach assault forces were to use live ammunition and, of course, come under live fire from attacking planes and ships while moving towards the shore. Smoke screens were to be used as well to cover troop movements up the beach and ground units were to call in support from fighter and medium bombers to destroy obstacles in their way.

Operation Tiger was planned from 22nd to the 29th April and involved troops stationed between Torbay and Plymouth,

the exercise taking place during the hours of darkness. Two landing craft full of troops were sunk and one was damaged causing the death of about 700 men — more than were killed on Utah beach itself. Such is the irony of war! The loss of the craft was critical to the *Overlord* assault lift as these craft were already in short supply. The Germans realised that they had sunk landing craft but fortunately did not conclude that they were part of a large military exercise.

Operation Fabius was planned along similar lines to *Tiger* and took place during the early days of May, 1944. The participating troops came from the Dorset area and comprised of units designated assault force "O". The objectives of the rehearsal were the same and the conditions under which it took place were to be as realistic as possible. The sea journey was also to be of the same

that is assault force "U". Major troop units involved were the 4th Infantry Division and the 82nd and 101st Airborne Divisions with support from other units. D-Day was planned for 27th April and the attack on the coast for first light of that day. The first object was to secure a beach-head and then make a rapid advance inland to secure certain objectives. The exercise finished on 29th April and the troops then returned to their various marshalling areas.

This first rehearsal was very successful and from it a number of co-ordinating lessons were learnt and then applied to the real invasion. One incident, however, marred this event. Two German E-boat flotillas totalling nine boats managed to pass the defending ships (there had been some last minute changes causing a weakness in the security) and stumbled on

length as that of the Channel crossing with troops and ships being accompanied by planes and ships.

Once again the Slapton Sands area came under attack procedure on fortified beach defences. This was immediately followed by waves of troops being brought into the area by landing craft and then staging an assualt on the beach and penetrating inland as fast as possible towards given objectives.

So the days of Slapton Sands usefulness as a training ground came to an end when the smoke had cleared and the noise and activity had finally ceased. All was now ready for the real invasion of Europe to take place within a month of the ending of the two exercises.

These five photographs show various aspects of the exercises in Start Bay. Landing craft can be seen coming in under a smoke screen, assembling off shore, then landing on the beach. A tractor is hauling craft up the steep pebble beach and soldiers can be seen cutting their way through the wire defences to form a beachead.

Germans Eluded Naval Patrols and Sank Landing Craft

SEVEN HUNDRED American soldiers were killed and three tank landing craft were sunk when, on April 28, 1944, German U-boats eluded the naval screen and attacked vessels taking part in the training off Slapton Sands for the D-Day landings in Normandy.

This was revealed officially for the first time on Saturday afternoon by the American General A. M. Gruenther, when he attended a ceremony to mark the tenth anniversary of the allied assault on Hitler's Atlantic wall.

This tragic happening was a well-kept secret—so well-kept, in fact, that after ten years astonishment was expressed even in official circles when General Gruenther's speech was published.

The facts were known to quite a number of local people, but they loyally and discreetly kept their mouths shut on the subject.

Earl Fortescue, the Lord Lieutenant, said later that it was "complete news" to him, the War Office knew nothing and U.S. Navy headquarters professed ignorance.

There was a reference in a dispatch from Admiral Sir Bertram Ramsay which referred to sinking of L.S.T. by enemy E-boats in Lyme Bay during an attack on "the last convoy to sail," but this does not appear to have been the same incident.

In the Drizzle

After a bad morning with fog and drizzle, the sun tried to break through the low clouds as people began to assemble at the obelisk erected near the ruins and rubble that were once the Slapton Sands Hotel. But thin drizzle closed down again, and spectators, as well as the Guard of Honour were thoroughly damped before the proceedings commenced.

It was in 1943 that the people of one of the most fertile areas of farm land in the country were evacuated so that it might be used as a training area for the United States Forces. They returned after the war to find buildings razed and land ravaged, but it was stated that the sacrifice had been instrumental in saving many lives when the Americans went ashore under enemy fire, benefiting by the lessons they had learned in South Devon.

Perhaps it was the weather or perhaps it was the rather bitter memory of the evacuation days, but there was only a thin attendance of local folk at the memorial yesterday.

Holiday-makers and officially-invited people swelled to some three or four hundred the numbers gathered around the hollow square formed by the Guard.

To the south was a detachment of seamen from the Royal Navy, spick and span in their summer rig, with long bayonets flashing and glinting as they sloped and presented arms with the precision of clockwork.

There was an assemblage of county and local dignitaries and officers of the Royal Navy, Royal Marines and Army with their ladies on the seaward side, when the Guard gave the general salute as General Gruenther arrived.

American Gratitude

After inspecting the Guard he was introduced to the assembly by Earl Fortescue, Lord Lieutenant of Devon. A short man, wearing the American dark khaki jacket and light trousers, the General stood at the base of the obelisk and made an informal, chatty little speech, with, albeit, a strong political flavour to give it bite.

He told of his first acquaintance with Devon as a schoolboy when, being asked to locate it, he described it as a province of England in the north of Scotland!

He expressed American gratitude for the facilities provided for their training during the last war by the people of the South Hams. He extolled N.A.T.O., saying it was necessary that the politicians should have adequate military backing, and he referred to another portion of the free world "disappearing into Soviet darkness as an outcome of the happenings of the last few days."

General Gruenther was thanked by Mr. R. W. Prowse, chairman of the Kingsbridge Rural District Council; naval ratings stationed at the halyards broke the Union Jack and the Stars and Stripes from flag-poles erected on either side of the memorial, the band played "The Star Spangled Banner" and "God save the Queen"—it was all over, sailors, and soldiers marched back to their buses, the elite hurried to their cars, and the locals strung out along the road on their way home to tea.

Two of the many interesting articles in local newspapers reporting events about the evacuation and its return to normal peacetime use.

BACK TO S.W. "BATTLE" AREA BY SEPTEMBER 15

PEOPLE WILL SOON BE GOING HOME—SOME TO A RUINED VILLAGE

MOST of the people evacuated from their homes seven months ago in order that an area in the south-west might be used as a battle-training ground for U.S. troops will be back again in a couple of months.

This applies to the villages of Blackawton, East Allington, Slapton, Strete, Stoke Fleming, Sherford and Stokenham, although there is little left of Strete.

At a meeting of the Rural District Council, on Friday, the Chairman said the authorities responsible for de-requisitioning the area were aiming at September 15 next as the time when most of the people might be back in their homes.

It was his own personal impression that certain villages will be re-occupied by that date, but others might not be ready until a few months later.

Speaking of a visit which he and other officials paid to the area last week, Mr. Prowse said at the outset he must say that the chief object of the visit was to inspect the roads.

Roads Passable

Generally speaking, the condition of the roads was not too bad. Every road was passable, but a good many of the roadside hedges and walls were down.

In most of the villages little damage could be seen. At one place there were one or two holes in the roof of the church.

The village of Strete, except for the building formerly used by the Women's Institute, had been burned down.

A clergyman member of the Council said he had heard that in one village a field had been used as a cemetery.

The Chairman replied that such a statement was entirely false, as were many of the stories in circulation relating to the damage done to property in the training area. He added:

"We only saw three signs of human habitation. Three vans. It was uncanny."

Little damage had been caused to the water supply and sewerage.

Repairing Houses

The plan for rehabilitating the area was to begin on the perimeter and to work inwards.

Extreme care was being taken to ensure that no live ammunition was left in the area.

Flying squads of men were being brought in to execute necessary repairs to houses, so that the people could occupy them as soon as possible.

The Vice-Chairman paid tribute to the great number of people from the area who had borne their hardships without making any complaint. He hoped the people affected would feel rewarded and be proud of the fact that they had played a real and personal part in the landings in Normandy.

Many of the troops who stormed the beaches of Normandy trained on beaches in this area. The people's sacrifice had not been in vain, and it might be comforting for them to know that.

People's Sacrifices

One member agreed with these remarks. On the other hand, the financial sacrifice which the evacuees had had to make could have been avoided.

Another member said they must not overlook the fact that the whole country had benefited by the sacrifices of these people, and, therefore, it was only fair that the whole country should put their hands in their pockets and help in the rehabilitation.

HELPING FARMERS

Hostel for Workers to Be Set Up

The County War Agricultural Executive Committee will assist in the rehabilitation of the farms and is setting up an office in the area for this purpose.

It is hoped to get most of the farmers back before the winter sets in, and the Committee will help them to the fullest possible extent with ploughing and in supplying labour.

Much work will have to be undertaken in clearing the land of any lurking danger from unexploded shell and the like before cultivation can be resumed.

A hostel for land workers is to be established, and a pool of W.L.A. girls and other labour will be available for farmers to draw upon when they require it.

U.S. Landings in Normandy, France, 6th June, 1944

The first troops from England to embark on this historic mission were the large American assault forces stationed along the coast of the West Country. *Force 'U'* from Salcombe, Dartmouth and Brixham, *Force 'O'* from Portland, Weymouth and Poole and the follow up *Force 'B'* from Plymouth and Falmouth were given orders to get under way on the 30th and 31st May and 1st June. All troops and equipment were on board by the 3rd June from which date the exact positions of attack were given although the precise day had still not been finalised due to very unsettled weather conditions.

Force 'U' was divided into twelve convoys which made their way along the coast towards Weymouth where *Force 'O'* was putting to sea in five convoys. Both assault forces followed a parallel route making for what was called the "spout"

an area of sea to be cleared of enemy mines through which all the five assault forces would have to pass before reaching the French coast (see map).

All the Chiefs of Staff were at headquarters in Portsmouth where up to the minute weather forecasts were coming in. During Sunday morning, 4th June, 1944, General Eisenhower decided to postpone the invasion for twenty-four hours although the two convoys were on course across the Channel. They were ordered to return to Weymouth Bay and await further instructions. On Sunday evening another weather report indicated an improvement in conditions upon which advice General Eisenhower gave the final order to launch the invasion in the early hours of Monday morning — *Operation Overlord* was under way!

The seventeen American convoys put to sea again and the British assault forces also got under way from various other points further up the Channel. American destroyers left their berths at Belfast, Ireland, on course for the battle zone and Airborne troops were boarding planes in many parts of England in readiness for their dropping points in Normandy now scheduled for the very early hours of Tuesday morning, 6th June, 1944.

While the U.S. Airborne troops were being dropped in the Cotentin area and British paratroopers near Caen, the invasion fleet was bringing the main body of the Allied armies to the Normandy shores. Mine sweepers cleared and marked ten lanes through enemy mines, fighter squadrons were above the convoys, there was still a low cloud level and the sea still very choppy. The crossing was uneventful and the Germans appeared to be unaware that anything unusual was taking place.

Approximately 13,000 bombs were dropped by 329 B-24 bombers on and around Omaha Beach and 293 planes softened up the defences on Utah Beach in a similar and more successful fashion as visibility was better in this area. At about 02.30 hours the headquarters ships were on station in the battle zone and troops were unloading into LCVP's that would take them to the beaches. At 05.45 the naval bombardment commenced from the destroyers and finished only minutes before the first troops from *Force 'U'* landed on Utah beach at 06.30. It was only a matter of minutes before the bombardment ceased that the defending Germans spotted the approaching forces.

It was too late to bring any major units up to defend the coast. The coastal batteries had already taken a hammering and now they were under close fire by the

first waves of infantry coming ashore followed by engineer and demolition parties. The Utah beach landings were well established after just three hours of fighting and tanks, vehicles and numerous support equipment was being quickly brought ashore from which point breakouts were taking place with relative ease. There were few casualties at this point and the plans were more or less put into operation as laid down. 23,250 men went ashore on the first day with 1,742 vehicles and 1,695 tons of stores.

However, the picture on the Omaha Beach was quite different. The bombing had been largely off target due to poor visibility, the infantry transports were swamped by high waves, a lot of equipment was lost and the first troops ashore were there mainly without support from howitzers and other guns. The German defences were still intact and consequently were able to pin down the infantry on the beach for much longer than was planned. Out of the five landings in the invasion this one was most difficult. Additional supplies had to be brought in and it was only after four or six hours of the most gruesome fighting that German bunkers were slowly put out of action and a beachhead was established. Some 3,000 died on this beach, the worst casualties of the whole operation.

Photographs:
The illustrations appearing on pages fourteen and fifteen show U.S. troops crossing the English Channel, landing, engaging in battle and sustaining casualties.

The South Hams To-day

Many years have passed since the last American troops left this part of South Devon for the Normandy beaches in June, 1944. It was not until well into the autumn of the same year that people started returning to their farms and houses, some finding their properties intact while others were grieved to find considerable damage both to buildings, walls, hedges and even outbuildings. In spite of much hardship compensation for damage was given and assistance offered towards moving and settling in again. The information centres were reopened and after the area had been cleared of mines and military debris many families were back in their former homes by the end of the year and a start had been made on farming the land.

Some buildings which had been completely destroyed were not rebuilt including the Royal Sands Hotel which stood close to the beach by the road going up to Slapton village. A few of the churches

had also been quite badly damaged and teams of experts were soon working on their restoration. Likewise the villages suffered, especially Strete although Torcross, in spite of its closeness to the sea, was relatively unharmed. Slapton Ley had been neglected, waterways choked with weeds and hardly any wildlife left except for rabbits which were found to be in great numbers over the whole area.

A granite obelisk now stands on the beach midway between Torcross and Strete which commemorates this episode in the life of the South Hams and the sacrifices made by the local people. It was unveiled on the 24th July, 1954, and presented by the United States of America. In spite of all the damage to buildings, trees, hedges and roads, hardly any scars remain from this period. There are occasional reports of shells being found and divers have located vehicles and other military equipment in the sea close to the shore.

Many visitors come to this area each year or pass through on their way to Kingsbridge or Salcombe. Some stop to read the lettering on the obelisk and ask questions about those far off days during the war. Many American visitors are curious about the area and some are pleased to find reminders such as the Normandy Inn, Blackawton, which contains photographs and some military relics.

The local people have not forgotten their part in the last war and the sacrifices they made in enabling this land to be used as a training battlefield in preparation for the Normandy invasion.

Photographs:
A close view of the lettering on the American obelisk at Slapton Sands.
A general view of the long beach at Slapton with Torcross in the foreground.
The Normandy Inn at Blackawton which was renamed after the war to commemorate the American exercises and landings in France.

Here ends the original book.

On the next page is a newspaper cutting from 2010 written by John Fairweather Tall. In this article he refers to this very book as being crucial in answering questions that had remained a mystery for many years.

We include this here as evidence of the importance of preserving local history and to celebrate the work of Arthur L Clamp in uncovering the past.

There then follows four pages of information not previously part of this book that celebrate the author's life, including a description of his publishing process in his own words. This was uncovered during the restoration project that has seen the republishing of many of the books that he published during his lifetime.

A military mystery

Research apparently reveals the disputed location of the great local Second World War controversy – Operation Tiger

by JOHN FAIRWEATHER-TALL

EVERY now and then one or the other of two particular local controversies crops up, with protagonists locked in mortal combat – fortunately only literary, writes John Fairweather-Tall, chairman of the Kingsbridge History Society.

One involves Alfred Lord Tennyson, made poet laureate in 1850, and the poem *Crossing the Bar*, described as 'the crown of his life's work'. The dispute, pursued for years, is over whether it was written of the Bar at Salcombe, or the Isle of Wight. Each has its proponents, none being prepared to give an inch of ground to those ranged against them.

The other controversy, evident in the pages of the *Gazette* in miles east of Slapton Sands, and who point to a US war memorial on Weymouth seafront which reads: '749 US Army/Navy personnel lost off Portland'. So who is right? What is needed to resolve the issue is someone transparently independent, with no axe to grind,

The view from the beach

taking objective research in original military archives. What, then, did such a researcher find? Embedded deep in his research is, perhaps, the key to the controversy.

The invasion, codenamed Operation Overlord, involved five assault forces,

Sands area came under attack procedure on fortified beach defences. This was immediately followed by waves of troops being brought into the area by landing craft and then staging an assault on the beach and penetrating inland as fast as possible towards

Contributed

Was this where Operation Tiger occurred?

recent weeks, concerns the site of a tragedy during the Second World War that marred an otherwise successful exercise, *Operation Tiger*. Two German E-boat flotillas totalling nine boats slipped past guard ships in the darkness – last-minute changes had led to a security lapse – and encountered the exercise at its height. They sank two landing craft full of troops and damaged a third, causing the death of some 700 men.

Such are the bare bones of the controversy, but where did the tragedy take place? That is the nub of the issue. Off Slapton Sands, say some, and point to a Sherman tank, recovered from the seabed, commemorating those who died. Farther eastwards, on the edge of the beach, is a granite obelisk, but this was presented by the American army as a thank you to those who vacated their homes to provide a practice area for the invasion proper. It does not commemorate *Operation Tiger*.

Others, equally strident in their tragedy claims, say it occurred off Portland, some 50 who is prepared to undertake completely objective research in original military archives. As *Exercise Tiger* involved American troops and landing craft, this research would involve American archives.

In fact just such research was done and published some 35 or more years ago. The author was the late Arthur Clamp, a local historian who lived in Elburton, Plymouth, whose carefully researched work was published under the title, *The American Assault Exercises at Slapton Sands, Devon, in 1944*. This is undated, but textual evidence suggests it to be around the mid-1970s.

'In the preparation of this account,' writes the author in his introduction, 'I was greatly helped by the American military archives in Washington, USA, from which source came the photographs. My thanks go to them and to many others working in Devon and London libraries who gave advice and time willingly.' That ticks all the boxes for the need of someone independent, with no axe to grind, under two of which were American and three British and other troops. The American forces, situated mainly in the West Country, were divided into two groups, designated 'U' and 'O', each commanded by an American Rear Admiral. Troops of assault force 'U' were stationed between Torbay and Plymouth, while assault force 'O' comprised troops stationed around the Dorset area (which includes Weymouth and Portland).

Now we come to the crux of the matter. *Operation Tiger* involved assault force 'U', began to move to its marshalling area on 22 April 1944, ready for its 'D-Day' rehearsal to begin on 27 April and end two days later. Shortly after the conclusion of *Oper-ation Tiger*, during the early days of May, another similar exercise took place. This involved assault force 'O', comprising troops from the Dorset area, and was code-named *Operation Fabius*. Arthur Clamp writes of this latter exercise (and, because of its importance in seeking to resolve the controversy, I quote him in full): 'Once again the Slapton given objectives.

'So the days of Slapton Sands' usefulness as a training ground came to an end when the smoke had cleared and the noise and activity had finally ceased. All was now ready for the real invasion of Europe to take place within a month of the ending of the two exercises.' From his account it is clear that there were two similar exercises, the first involving troops from the area between Torbay and Plymouth, and code-named *Operation Tiger*. It was during this exercise, so the research indicates, that the tragedy occurred involving the loss of some 700 troops. The second exercise involved troops stationed in the Dorset area, and was code-named *Operation Fabius*. There appears to be no reference in the US military archives to any tragedy in this latter exercise similar to that of the earlier one.

The tragedy was such a well-kept secret that, according to a local newspaper of 1954, when an American General mentioned it during a ceremony to mark the tenth anniversary of

Top-secret letter about the exercise

D-Day, the Lord Lieutenant admitted later that it was 'complete news' to him. The War Office and top-secret letter dated April 19 detailing US Navy headquarters also said they knew nothing of it. Little wonder, then, that confusion and controversy still reign. The report of this ceremony included reference to a dispatch from Admiral Sir Bertram Ramsay, Naval Commander in Chief of the Allied Naval Expeditionary Force for the invasion, which mentioned a sinking of LST (Landing Ship, Tank) by enemy E-boats in Lyme Bay. However, this was during an attack on 'the last convoy to sail', not during *Operation Tiger*, and, according to the report, 'does not appear to have been the same incident'. It has also to be said that in neither of these exercises, *Tiger* or *Fabius*, is there any mention of tanks being involved. The top-secret letter dated April 19 detailing events of the rehearsed 'D-Day' on April 27 and the subsequent two days, mentions only simulated landings by Airborne Divisions and the advance of an Infantry Division. There is no mention of any armoured force. There is also a picture of soldiers cutting a way through barbed wire defences. This would be a needless task if tanks were on hand to do the job in a fraction of the time.

Unless objective research from military archives yields compulsive evidence to the contrary, it would seem that, wherever the Sherman tank came from, it was not from *Operation Tiger*.

Arthur L. Clamp – the man behind the books

Arthur Leslie Clamp was a man of boundless energy with a passion for helping others, particularly through his love of history. A printer by trade, he started his career in a printing company before moving his family from Exeter to Plymouth to teach at the Plymouth College of Art and Design, where he eventually became the Head of the Printing Department.

A Devoted Family Man

Arthur with his five children.

Despite his love of teaching, Arthur prioritised his family, always making it home by 5:30pm for tea. He and his wife, Rosemary, raised five children: Susan, Angela, Elizabeth, David, and Steven. Arthur would often combine his love of family and history by taking his children on Sunday walks, encouraging them to appreciate historical monuments by taking photos or making crayon rubbings of gravestones for his books. The family home at 203 Elburton Road was a hub of activity, with a large garden, featuring a two-storey fort and a makeshift swimming pool.

A Lifelong Learner and Adventurer

Arthur's thirst for knowledge extended beyond history to a deep curiosity about the world. He was passionate about exploring different cultures, traditions, and cuisines, often taking advantage of his long summer holidays as a teacher to travel to places like India, Russia, South America, the middle east and the USA, sometimes bringing one of his children along. This adventurous spirit even influenced his home life, as seen by the short-lived family tradition of steam-cooking vegetables after a trip to Iceland.

History is a prominent feature of family days out

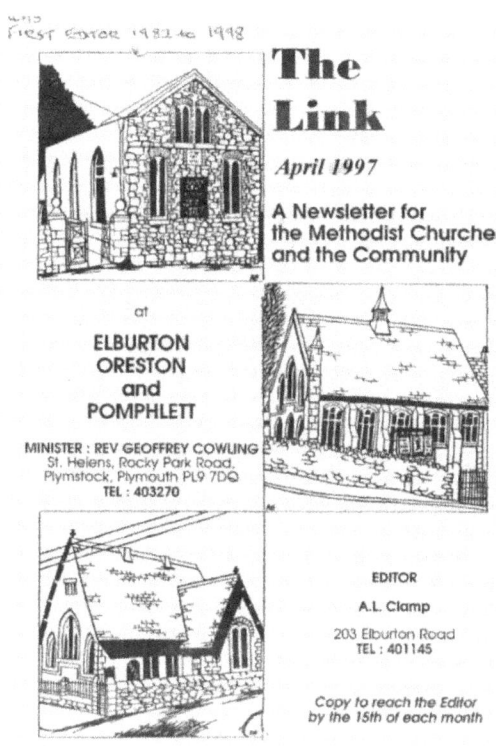

Community and Philanthropic Spirit

His commitment to serving others was evident in his long-standing involvement with the Elburton Methodist Church. He was the Sunday School Superintendent for over 15 years and served as the editor of the wider church's monthly newsletter, "The Link," for a similar duration. After Rosemary's very sad passing, Arthur later remarried and, following a chance encounter with a professor from India, established a connection with a missionary school in Chennai. Together with his new wife, Christine, he co-founded a "Sponsor a Child's Education" program that continues to this day.

*Pictured left – The cover of 'The Link' complete
with hand drawn sketches of each church by Angela
Below right – Arthur Clamp promoting his latest book
Below left – Arthur at home with his first wife, Rosemary
Below centre – Arthur on holiday with his second wife, Christine*

A Legacy of Learning and Positivity

Arthur's greatest passion was history, which he brought to life through tireless research, documentation, and the many books he authored. He was driven by a need to "never be stuck in a rut," constantly seeking new experiences, meeting new people, and expanding his knowledge. With a positive attitude and a great sense of humour, he was always ready to help others, leaving a lasting impact on his family and community. His children, Susan, Angela, Elizabeth, David, and Steven, remember him with love and gratitude.

David Clamp, 2025

A Legacy of Local History

Below is the story of how Arthur L Clamp began writing books, in his own words, drafted shortly before he passed away in 2001. I have only made minor alterations to this text, correcting grammatical errors that he did not survive to correct himself. When I first discovered this text, I was shocked to see my name mentioned. It seems that, unbeknownst to me, I shared my first PC with him. I suspect he used it during the day when I was at school, although I do have one memory of sitting with him and showing him how it worked. It has been a pleasure to pick up where he left off and see his books republished and redistributed, and to know that I was part of the story, even back then. It was also fascinating to discover that his pricing structure matches the way I have tried to price the books, with a third going to local sellers and the rest covering printing costs with a little left over for my expenses.

I am his eldest grandson, and it is a privilege to curate his legacy, which we are calling 'The Clamp Collection'. The very last line of the text originally reads "The following pages list all the titles." Sadly, that page is missing and we have no record of all the books he published and knowing that some of those were researched by other authors makes the process of finding them even harder. I look forward to one day completing the collection and seeing them all available again. And maybe, one day, I'll even start writing my own to add to the series. For now, here is his story in his own words.

Steven Gibson, 2025

Writing and Publishing Booklets on Local Topics and Areas

I started this interest in either 1968 or 1969 when living in Woodford. I had by these dates established the Department of Printing and I think I must have been looking for something different to do. The first titles were of A5 size proofed from type set at Clarke, Doble and Brendon, Ltd., Plymouth printers, and then made up into pages and printed at Sawtell and Neilson, Ltd., Totnes.

Then began a slow process of getting them out to shops, etc. which proved to be more time consuming and difficult than actually researching, writing and getting the books into print. However, I persisted and opened a business account with Barclays Bank on the Broadway. I was advised to give it a title so I called it "Westway Publications". There came along another problem, one of storage of paper and finished books which was solved when the family moved to Elburton in 1970.

I changed the printer to Penwell, Ltd., Callington, Cornwall, as he was then just setting up himself and his prices seemed very reasonable. I did not get any of the printers to make up the complete books. I hand folded the flat printed sheets, stitched the books on a small manual table stitcher and trimmed them in a small hand turned guillotine which I bought from someone in Penzance for £40. It was brought up in a van.

The trouble and time going to and fro to Callington was too much so I transferred the printing to PDS Printers, Prince Rock, Plymouth, and I have been with them ever since. Now they are at Plympton which is easy to reach and they fold the flat sheets which was turning out to be a long chore which only saved a small part of the printing costs.

All my first titles were written by myself. I took the photographs and developed them in the loft of the house, the type was set by now on a computer situated in the house at Elburton from which I had collected photographic lengths of text to cut up and law down as pages.

At some point I decided that I would do my own film processing of lith film so I bought a large second hand process camera from Kingsbridge and learnt through trial and error to make line negatives of the text and halftone negatives of the illustrations which proved more difficult than I anticipated. The main problem was trying to keep the developer in the large dish at the correct temperature as any change would affect the developing time. I replaced this old camera with a brand new one bought from Croydon, Surrey, costing £900. This has turned out to be a great asset cutting out an expensive part of the printer's costs and one crucial aspect of the work which I could control.

By the middle 1970s there were many outlets I had contacted in Plymouth, up to Dartmoor, Exeter, around to Torbay, Totnes, Dartmouth and the South Hams. The market for local books was much greater than I had first thought and through getting to know many local people undertaking research themselves had the chance to help and make up books for other people who had in most instances, got together a collection of photographs with some text in a rather muddled way. Through my experience in print I was able to shape up their work and get it into print and in every case I had to pay the printer and let the person have the royalties. In the majority of titles produced in this manner this was another way of producing titles and it did give some profit to my work. However, I must say that in a few cases I lost out by either the other person getting the numbers wrong, not returning any monies from stock I delivered or they thought that more of their books should have been sold.

The print run was usually 1,000 copies and from time to time I have had reprints of 250 copies. It took about ten years to clear the first print run so I always had large stocks in the garage, workshop, etc. The numbers sold during the early years was about 7,000 copies a year increasing to around 9,000 copies and for the whole of the enterprise about 500,000 have been sold. The booklets have become part of the local scene and many people collect them, shops regularly order copies and I go around certain areas month by month restocking or replacing titles as necessary.

During the past year or so I have started setting the text on a Packard Bell PC, something which I should have done some years back. I share it with Steven Gibson, my grandson. There appears to be no end to the market for local books, but I could not earn a regular income because of the long time it takes to sell stock.

However, now exceeding 100 titles made up mainly of A4 twenty-four page booklets, some folded guides, with selling prices set with a third going to the shop which is the trade custom, the original idea has been quite successful and could go on for ever.

Apart from monetary benefits, however spasmodically these might be, I have learnt a lot myself, met many interesting people and have become part of the local scene with requests to give talks and to advise people about getting into print.

Arthur L Clamp, 2001

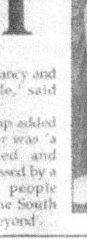

This newspaper article, published by the Evening Herald on 17th August 2001, forms a good record of his life. Just as he encourages us to learn more about local history, we encourage you to learn a little about him. For that reason, we have included these pages at the back of all the most recently republished books, in honour of his memory and recognition of his contribution to the community.

www.ingramcontent.com/pod-product-compliance
Lightning Source LLC
Chambersburg PA
CBHW061409070526
44584CB00031B/4197